WHITE INK STAINS

Eleanor Brown was born in 1969 and lived in Scotland until the age of 12. She studied English Literature at York. After graduating she worked variously as a waitress, barmaid, legal secretary, and minutes secretary, to be able to work also as a poet and translator of poetry. In 2001-02 she was Creative Writing Fellow at the Universities of Glasgow and Strathclyde. She now lives, works, writes, sings (alto) and dances (Argentine tango) in Sheffield.

Her debut collection, *Maiden Speech*, published by Bloodaxe in 1996, was shortlisted for the *Mail on Sunday*/John Llewellyn Rhys Prize. She was one of the five poets featured in Bloodaxe's 1997 New Blood promotion. Her second collection, *White Ink Stains*, was published by Bloodaxe in 2019.

Two of her works for theatre were commissioned and produced by Inigo Theatre company: a verse adaptation of Sophocles's *Philoctetes*, performed at the Cockpit Theatre, London in 1997; and the first version of Frank Wedekind's *Franziska* to be published in English, performed at the Gate Theatre, London, in 1998, and published by Oberon Books.

More recently, in 2014 she led workshops for the University of Sheffield's French department, on translating poems by Baudelaire and Gautier in the context of musical settings by Vierne and Berlioz to produce singable versions of the texts.

Since 2013 she has worked with the support and sponsorship of the Reading Sheffield oral history project, a grant from which funded a writing week. Some of the poems in *White Ink Stains* were presented at the University of Roehampton's 2016 Oral History Conference Beyond Text in the Digital Age? in a paper discussing voice in oral history and voice in poetry.

ELEANOR BROWN

White Ink Stains

BLOODAXE BOOKS

ISBN: 978 1 78037 494 9

First published 2019 by
Bloodaxe Books Ltd,
Eastburn,
South Park,
Hexham,
Northumberland NE46 1BS,

www.bloodaxebooks.com
For further information about Bloodaxe titles
please visit our website and join our mailing list
or write to the above address for a catalogue

Supported using public funding by
ARTS COUNCIL
ENGLAND

Cover design: Neil Astley & Pamela Robertson-Pearce.

Printed in Great Britain by Bell & Bain Limited, Glasgow, Scotland, on
acid-free paper sourced from mills with FSC chain of custody certification.

CONTENTS

For Mary Grover

Representation

All small poor mousy lonely young
displaced or dispossessed
bookish resentful highly strung
ambitious ardent oppressed
acute impatient outspoken shy
perceptive hungry mistreated
scrupulous introspective wry
morally overheated
avid imaginative plain
passionate angry clever
girls are depending on you, Jane.
Be Jane for us all forever.

She's Going in an Office like her Daddy

My father was a clerk
In a small steelworks
There was only the manager and him there
Until the manager's son came home
From university
And then he was there too
A bit of a spare part
As they say
All he'd do, he'd go to the library
Over the road
Come back with a big pile of books
Sit with his feet up on the desk
Reading them
I thought I could do that

When I was very small
My mother walked me to the library
A mile and a half each way
And uphill home
One time I said why don't we take a tram
For the fun of it
But she was angry and sad
She said no, we're walking

When I was twelve, thirteen
And the manager was away
My father would take me into work
I'd sit and play
On the beautiful big old black
Imperial typewriter
I remember
Being taken into the forge
With the hammers banging away,
Seeing the horses,
Writing just whatever I wanted

Twenty-two years a stockbroker's typist
For love of that old Imperial.
And because one time I asked
To take a tram home from the library
But mother hadn't had the two pence for it,
Not the penny ha'penny for herself
Nor the half penny for me.

This Is My Own Bit of Thing

I've travelled the world twice over, met famous saints and sinners,
Poets and artists, kings and queens, all stars and hopeful beginners;
I've been where no one's been before, learned secrets from writers
    and cooks –
Always on a library ticket to the wonderful world of books.

These are some poems I've written
Some I remembered or found
Some we would chant in the classroom
Some in the playground

Some that the high wind scribbled
Across the fretful sky
When I ran and ran on the moor
Not knowing why

Some in the slanting script
Of my lifelong friend the rain
One I wrote in my breath
On a window pane

Many that I discovered
Alone in Porter Clough
Some among Mother's recipes –
Not enough –

Carefully pencilled, then inked,
In her scrupulous schoolgirl hand
Tucked between pickles and pies
In no man's land

And I think that an education
Is not knowing facts from a book
It's knowing what you're looking for
And how to look

Dawn break through the leaves in Rivelin
Cloud rift at Stanage Edge
A bumblebee on a dry stone wall
Wrens in a hedge

Limitless changeable moorland skies,
That's the heaven for me;
But if I did have to be shut in –
A good library.

Appetite

Book-hungry teenage girl, great ravenous
word-eating eyes, amazing stamina
for nothing but to lie in bed and read –
omnivorous of print, devouring gaze
insatiable for all the big fat works,
yes all of Dickens, Eliot and James,
now Tolstoy, Dostoevsky, Zola, Proust:
keep it up, gents and ladies, churn it out,
as long as I'm pupating in my bed
sixteen years old with nothing else to do,
there's no Leviathan of literature
I'll be defeated by, no Behemoth
of books can make me say 'Too much for me.'
Something got into me that can't get out.
Something got hold of me that won't let go.

What Would You Put Dracula Under?

I was seventeen when a curate came to our church.
He lent me these books I've never seen anywhere since
and I've looked for them often.
Not spiritual. They weren't spiritual.
Not magic, either; like magic, but not.
Bit like a Dracula type?
What would you put Dracula under?
Not horror. Not gothic either. Weird.

I've often asked my friends, because we used to go
to his flat on Sunday evening after church
for coffee, a bit like a youth club,
but I was the only one
who ever took these books home
so none of my friends remember them.
None of them even remember him that much.

I think they were unpleasant things.
But once I started reading I was hooked.
I read all through the night, feeling sort of sick,
and took one back to bring another home.
He's an old man now, in his 80s,
he ended up some big shot at the Minster.
I saw him a while ago, and I was going to
ask him about these books.
It's very strange
I can't get hold of them anywhere.

I read too many too fast; I was hooked.
I couldn't stop.
One night I turned my head to see the clock
and there was a dirty great spider,
right there on my pillow. Him,
watching me read.
Watching me be seventeen and scared.

Heroes I

My father came from an academic family
and used to tell us stories
about the Greek heroes
which led on to the *Iliad*
and the *Odyssey*.
He was also a great fan of the *Idylls of the King*,
and we loved those stories, we would read them
over and over. The whole thing.
When we came to do Tennyson
I found I could recite whole gobs of it off by heart
before we even started.
I still can, to this very day.

Now I always loved
Wuthering Heights and I always loved
Jane Eyre. I've had various copies of those
because they fall to bits in the end, don't they.
Every time they film a new version I re-read it,
to make sure I've not gone daft;
and I'm never satisfied with Rochester.

Because if you read her description of Rochester –
not nice-looking, not very tall,
stocky, swarthy and yet
somehow magnetic – then all those
heart-throbs they get to play Rochester,
they're nothing of the sort.

And not only that.
They introduce all that sex into it;
and I mean
Charlotte Brontë
just doesn't go in for that, does she.

You can think what you like,
but she never mentioned it.

Girls Don't Need to be Educated, They Get Married

Which, even then there wasn't any law.
You're not obliged to; nobody can make
you say I do. You mightn't meet the one;
he mightn't ask; and even if he did
and you accepted, which you mightn't choose,
well – you could lose your husband various ways:

downed off a ladder, seeing to a slate;
drowned in the bath after a heart attack;
stricken: by lightning out on Beauchief course,
or shellfish in a Filey caravan;
another woman or another man;
a morning in his 40s when he walks
out of the door and never does come back.

You join the library, you educate
yourself, read everything. One day you gaze
transfixed at him transfigured, wonder who's
the angry stranger wrestling the lid
of your green compost bin on your front lawn,
dough-faced and pointless as a William Blake
angel. It's what an education's for.

Location Location Location

Go to church, then. A good one, with pillars
like oaks long since stricken to silence,
stone still.
Fan vaulting for foliage, fretwork
screens and stained glass to splinter and scatter
sunspill.
Dust suspended in downpours of darkslaying
gold, and a good god onlooking his
goodwill
far off at one end; at the other, your father,
dear, late, and delighted, patiently waiting
until
you arrive, like a column of light with a woman in,
fragrant and fresh, unfurling flower
and frill.

Between dad and god, like a david between two goliaths,
the man you'll have married the moment you murmur
you will.

Let a fanfare be flung at the poised air
like a challenge, the whole church shiver
and thrill.
Now walk: the way forward is wide
enough, and the priest prepared to perform
with skill
the regular rites as he finds them written.
Let scripture be read, receive sacraments, eat, drink
your fill;
be perfectly sure of yourself and it all; be good
and ready to sign when they bring you
the bill.

Honeymoon

Married in 1948. I had
the most exquisite nightdress, sort of like
a Greek goddess, and dressing gown to match.
They were the loveliest things I'd ever owned.
During the weeks before the wedding I'd
unwrap them from their tissue paper, hold
them up against myself and slowly sway
a sideways figure-of-eight. Didn't have
a full-length looking-glass and didn't dare
steal to my parents' room to look in theirs.

We went away on honeymoon, the boat
to France and then by train to Switzerland.
I hadn't brought enough to read. A kind
lady lent me a silly magazine:
the actress Lana Turner, 28,
was married for the fourth time, her trousseau
reported to have cost ten thousand pounds.
I gazed out of the window doing sums;
how many pairs of stockings must she have?
how many nightdresses and dressing gowns?

My husband hadn't long been back from war
and – sort of totally exhausted – so
he slept a lot, in the warm weather. Well,
and I was very bored. But luckily,
luckily in this little Swiss hotel
there were a few English books. I was so
pleased to have them. I'd have read anything
(always somebody worse off than you
in a Thomas Hardy). Nobody says,
pack enough books to last the honeymoon.

Nice Murders

Mother liked reading, especially,
she lived to 97, so she liked reading.
She liked reading what she called nice murders.
We often laughed, me sister and I,
we'd say Oh, that was a nice murder,
Mum would have liked that one.

I was young, I was very young, till I was nineteen.
We weren't like they are today.
I wasn't allowed to do things. I mean,
the night of the blitz I wanted to go to a dance
but my parents said no, and that was it.
You see, they said no.

I remember that night, there was the blitz.
I walked into work the next day.
When I saw all the mess, I just walked all the way home.
There was nowhere to go to work.
And I remember my father never talked
about the Great War.

I disposed of a lot of my books.
Nobody wants the embroidery books,
they don't do it today.
I rang my daughter in Australia;
she said Mam,
I haven't time to embroider.

Probably at the end of a working day,
once you'd got the children to bed;
my husband would sit in one chair,
I'd sit in another, and well,
sometimes you'd talk the whole evening.
And I'd knit and sew as well.

I'm reading books properly now.
In earlier days I'd be impatient to skip to the end,
find out what happened.
But now I read every word.

Damsel-fly

If Nana's darning needle
turned bright electric blue
and, of a sudden, breathed
why then what might she do

might craft herself four wings
from scraps she found of net
threaded with power and purpose,
but ain't seen nothing yet:

might penetrate the tangles
of rickrack ribbon trim
to pick two glitter bead-eyes
out of the button tin.

Sights now; flexes; shoots
out of the sewing box
to live a dazzling huntress
by river-tumbled rocks;
slim swift blue dart of danger,
far from the undarned socks.

The Dressmaker

Me mother were ambitious
And me Dad a traveller
They couldn't build that new estate
Quick-smart enough for her.

And Dad he died when I were two
Then it were hard for us
I wasn't very clever
So I failed eleven plus

They asked us what we liked to do
Me mother spoke for me
'She likes to sew' – 'Then she should go
In the shirt factory.'

And I were furious! For that
I could nor would not bear.
Oh, I came home and angry-cried
'I will not go in there.'

I got a real dressmaking job
I loved it every bit
But shop were gutted out by fire
When next door shop got hit

Me and me friends, we danced all night
All day we worked and learned
I took home to me widowed mum
Two thirds of what I earned

But there's a lot I can't recall.
I suffered from depression.
'Roll up! Donate your living brain
To the medical profession!'

'Electric shock those demons out!'
'Keep calm and carry on!'
So scorched and doped, I've half a mind –
The other half is gone.

Old Meg she's still a Gypsy, though,
And Love's still not Time's fool –
They never could burn out what got
Burnt into me at school.

A Tragedy on Every Page

When I was at junior school we'd got
a very far-seeing teacher
she had a little library and we used to borrow
those books from her bookshelf
we were supposed to write
a commentary about what we thought
Swallows and Amazons and the William books
the Katy books and *Anne of Green Gables*

When I was 22 and married we rented
a part-furnished cottage out in Derbyshire
it was an hour's walk to the nearest bus stop
but the mobile library would come
right out to all those isolated places.
I can't remember any of the titles but I remember
this one and it was really tragic
my husband came home from work
and says to me, Who's upset you?
Who's upset you?

When they were wanting to train mature people for teaching
I'd still got a little boy, hadn't I, the one born
later than the others and my mother went mad
You've got three children here, and there you are going to college!
I thought Mother, I'm nearly 45
I decided to do this A-level in English Literature
I sort of got that thirst for knowledge again

When I went up to the college I was nearly
up the wall I was so frustrated
I was getting
my mind was working on the wrong things, in
a black hole. I'd be putting the washing
in the washing-machine thinking, now,

he says this essay's got to have
a good start – a wholesome middle – and a good end.
I'd be planning it in me head and my mind
worked

It was life-saving, that.
Well. It didn't do me marriage any good
but it kept me sane.

Fast-talking Girl

You be the guy with the trustworthy chin
that takes on the bad guys called Knuckles and Earl,
won't sell what they want, won't buy what they sell,
and tells the bent governor he'll see him in hell;
you be him: every true story you're in,
I'll be the fast-talking girl.

What I can do, I can talk
21 to the dozen as though I was born to it pal,
like a champion barrow-boy hawking
for gold; half a chance and I'll talk
all four legs off the donkey and every dumb beast in this yard
full of honking and bleating and squawking,
you bet; stick with me, I can talk
us a mile and a half into trouble before you draw breath
to say darling, let me do the talking
this time – a blue streak? I could talk
you a streak every shade of the rainbow and several besides
with a pop like the winner uncorking
the bottle of fizz I would talk
you a fountain that never ran dry, if you gave me the grin

that says Attagirl, go ahead, tell
the dumb suckers they kept the dumb shell,
ate the oyster and threw out the pearl.
Just you be the guy with the go-ahead grin,
and any true story you want to be in,
I'll be your fast-talking girl.

The Empress and the Golden Swan

My mother didn't read to me, she hadn't got time for that, there were eight of us! Well, they went in for 'em in those days, didn't they. I wasn't clever enough to pass the scholarship exam, as it was called. I drew a part in *A Midsummer Night's Dream*, I was – who is it? Gets turned into a donkey. J.B. Priestley, I think it's him, I went up into the Dales with me sister, she lives at York, and I think we went where J.B. Priestley's buried. *The Ragged-trousered Philanthropist* I read quite recently, I got it out of a charity shop up where we have the caravan, and I think that's where it still is. He was quite a gentleman wasn't he, supposed to be, and he was going among these working class chaps. That H. Rider Haggard sort of story is nice for a change from romantic novels, a bit more exciting. Oh now: he was a sort of spy thing during the war against the Nazis, yes, because they capture his girlfriend, and they keep her to get to him, because they know he'll come for her, to get her out. And he does! I've seen a lot of that, Agatha Christie, on television. With that David Suchet as Poirot. Did you know they used to live at the Railway Hotel in Sheffield? Parents kept it. The best one I thought who did Sherlock Holmes was, I think his name was Brett. Jeremy Brett. He committed suicide, didn't he. I like Wodehouse, I like Blandings. The pig. Ever so funny about this pig, it's called the Empress of Blandings; but the television thing they made of it, there weren't enough of the pig. It wasn't good enough. You never heard about the Empress. Oh yes, I've had quite a lot of their books, Mills and Boon, from the bookshop on the road. *Lady Chatterley's Lover* I've read both versions of, because it was banned, and there was one printed with bits cut out. A lot cut out. And then somebody lent me the actual one, and it was entirely different, wasn't it. In a way, you can sort of imagine... Him. Being so rough and ready. And she's so elegant, supposed to be, in't she. The lady. And of course, she's frustrated because she's not getting anything. And her husband's the lord of the manor, and he's paralysed from the war. First war. Actually, it was me husband I got it through, it had been going round their office and he brought it me from there. We went to Newcastle. And we went to somewhere else. A house. Bowes Museum. I think it was some French people, as a matter of fact, but it was a lovely house and we went round it. And when we came downstairs, there was a golden swan at the bottom of the staircase, and at four o'clock every day it made tea. Mechanical like. And we all stood around on the staircase watching it. No. I didn't want any, actually. I'd had enough. After the war when me mum and dad used to go out with some friends on a Saturday night, Norah and I had to look after the youngest ones. Norah had Dorothy, who was about two, and I had to look after the baby. So I'd had enough of it. And Bill wasn't bothered either, because he was the youngest of nine.

Verbatim

We both like well-written
books because I think sometimes the, the
peers people speak in today, they
they don't sort of fickle any extra

words

which we used to do at
work when I was a young
lass there was a
woman who was a wonderful
person she read
everything before her and every
day I can see she'd come in and say

a word

and I had to memorise this
word and it'd be a long
word that'd fit a certain
subject I can't just think off the
top you know

it really got, taught me a
lesson to look for and I used to then get the
dictionary out you know start looking for

words

that I'd battle her with
I never did, like, but that was the
idea behind it

Friends

JESSIE: I was an only child, quite lonely I think
and got lost in books. I read, I suppose
out of boredom, but then
I would be involved; then I would be
the character in the book.

EDITH: I used to read during my lunch hour.
Very unsociable, but that's what I did.

JOYCE: I used to like poetry as well. I'm sorry.
Well, I've never been very good at making friends
but I more or less liked to go to the theatre
so I always found the, went to the plays
on my own
and I loved going to the opera
more than anything
when the opera came to Sheffield
I'm sorry.
Am I boring?

VIOLET: I used to get to school early
and sit alone and read for pleasure there
before I had to go down to the classroom
chose poetry for prizes when I got them
it was at the school library that I sought out
these bits that I got fond of
I'm so grateful for those books.

JOAN: I was an only child, and I think…if you get tired
of playing with friends
or you haven't got any friends
you've *always* got a friend in a book.

OLIVE: They were real people to me
         you can *see* Jane, in the window seat
         hiding from her cousin, reading the book
         maybe I was a bit like that
         I never thought about it before
         hiding away, reading your book
         not wanting anybody to find you.

Sleepovers

My parents were always busy,
they never did read to me.
I was a very poor reader
and not quick to learn.
The letters were acrobatic imps
writhing beneath my eyes, they were
black insects, skittering away
from my comprehension, laughing
ha–ha–he–ah–ha.

Miss Firvale doubted I would ever
amount to much. But I had a girlfriend
that lived next door.
We were born four days apart and we grew up
like sisters. We used to have sleepovers.

One of my greatest joys
was to lie in bed with her
while she read to me. Snow White
and Rose Red, safe all night
on the cliff edge, watched by the angel;
safe in the single bed, with the rise and fall
of the beloved voice,
familiar rhythms of our favourite tales.
The letters behaved for her, you see.
I wished those nights would last forever.

Yes, that was my greatest joy:
for her to read to me.
I found out in later years that I'm
dyslexic. I didn't know at the time.
It was a thing that was unheard of.

The one that I came in with

Though each star is a tiny anemone,
and the night is a long cool drink
with a bright, semicircular, lemony
moon on its glassy brink;

though I'm rising in antisociety
with a good head start on the pack,
kissing airy goodbyes to sobriety,
singing 'You wait here, I'll be back';

though the moon's a curved blade, though it whittles
away the soft stuff of my mind;
though my principles scatter like skittles,
and the best judge I'll be has resigned;

stuck for words, liquor-stricken, moonstruck,
or spoiling for love or a fight,
I'll be sticking with you, and with luck
I might be a lady tonight.

Good Smells

Father kept chickens and Mother
took in lodgers   we weren't very well off then
at all   *Humpty Dumpty* smells of raw grain
she popped me in a tram and took me to the Storrs school

They had to sell up the family firm
The Little Red Hen smells of iron filings
started in the seventeenth century
there was no way we could make a living

In the war the teacher came round our houses
four or five of us went up to the fishmonger's
on Greystones Road   they had more room there
Alice's Adventures in Wonderland smell of mackerel

I think we did more reading because
on a dark night you couldn't go out to play
The Forsyte Saga smells of cottage pie
he liked his *Morning Telegraph*   she knitted

I wanted to be a librarian   I don't know why
I changed my mind   we did *Merchant of Venice*
I must say
I understand about the pound of flesh

now   we didn't have a bookcase just a thing
a bookrest a shelf   *Il Penseroso* and t'other one
L'Allegro   smells of pink carbolic soap
posh universities needed you to have

Latin to study modern social science
Sheffield were the only one would have me
The Beveridge Report smells of the warm
vinegar breath of the West Street chip shops

Assistant Librarian

Because I am one of an orderly race,
a regular, hushing, labelling breed
that sows in rows in a quiet place
a systematically indexed seed;
bespectacled, strict but not unkind,
cardiganed, widely but not well read,
they think they can read my orderly mind
and the regular thoughts in my quiet head.

Well maybe they can and maybe they can't.
I've been coming in here since I was ten.
Prim and trim as a spinster aunt
I'd sit in a corner and read about men:
Lives of the Great Composers. I'm
not much of a one for light romance,
bodies and bodices, untrue crime,
victims of fictional circumstance.

Biography, travel, anything else…
Everything, really, booking them in,
stamping them out, stacking the shelves,
checking the murmur that swells to din
if library-users are left unchecked.
A boy from our class who went away
to Bangor did better than you'd expect;
he's famous now in the USA,

composer conductor. Not relevant;
I looked it up on the Internet.
Covers do matter. The time we spent
replacing slimy old leatherette!
There was a sack for the Discard books
(but first you had to rip them apart
which is harder work than perhaps it looks
if the binding's strong, and you're sick at heart

because nothing's wrong with the words inside,
it's still all there, the spine still straight)
worn, torn or soiled, the violet-eyed
heroine's hairstyle out of date –
quietly earning my regular wages
I grasped the covers and bent them back,
pulled out the middles, ripped up the pages
and tossed them into the Discard sack.

Wannabe 1938

This is the time when I get the ticket
for the public library
and Dad is saying
you must never let a library book go overdue
you must always take them back on time.

So off I go to Rotherham library
which I love going to:
it is like a cathedral, all hushed
and quiet with wooden floors;
everything gleaming, polished,
and nobody speaks to you.

And the best books, that I read
over and over again, I love so much
that when I travel to school
I secretly look at the people on the bus
and fix them into the books.

All the books are still
hardback books and I love them.
It smells of polish and hardback books
and I want to be a librarian
so much, I would do any work,
I would do anything to work
in a library.

Unsatisfied Requests

Of course, no one is computerised.
Not the County Bibliographer
riffling her card index
with such swift fingers; not Purchasing,
with her pink chits and rubber stamps.
Not even the Manor Clinic next door
with its shut-faced nurses.
I deal with the unsatisfied requests
from all the libraries.

Twentieth-century librarians,
we have to be the internet
until it gets invented.
Walking towers of knowledge,
we hold it all in our heads.
Somebody tells us a title, we put
our hand straight on it. Unsatisfied
requests just take a little longer; I'll get
your book for you one way or another.

Gatekeepers too: we have a back room
of censored and restricted texts, the books
on sex, childbirth,
contraception, disease,
which are not on the open shelves.
Just wooden blocks, with paper labels on.
you want the book, you bring me the block,
I fetch it from our store.

Next door down is the shut-faced clinic.
So of course the ladies,
one by one the pregnant ladies, the girls,
the others, come in for those books;
each wordlessly holding out her wooden block
to ask a civil servant for a book
she might perhaps better have had sooner.

All the Little Mermaids

Prepare to be slapped with the fact of your
own ordinariness. She won't look up
from what she's knitting, or her dirty cup;
your taut face won't intrigue her any more
than any of the others. *Well, which is it?*
Something you can't live with, or something you
can't live without? she'll ask, knit one purl two
knit one, *or is this just a social visit?*

She won't be listening while you explain
the intricate predicament. She'll wait
for your stammering halt, then indicate
a dog-eared price list. You will pay. *The pain,*
she'll say, *is sharp at first, but you can learn*
how to seem unaffected. There will be
no anaesthetic, and no guarantee.
For me, it was soon over: a thin burn,

a thread of fire she fed into my throat
to hook the voice out. Afterwards I bled
a little, and it hurt to turn my head
in order not to look at it, afloat
in a cracked basin. Outside, the old wives
muttered and nudged each other as I passed –
she's not the first, and she won't be the last –
because I walked as though I walked on knives.

Fen Jenny

O will you tread the causeway
By night and all alone?
Then do not wait the count of three
On any stepping stone
Nor do not let the moonlight gleam
Upon your ankle bone

Her arms are long, her hands are strong
Her fishbone teeth are many
Her gaze is like the winter moon
And hungry is Fen Jenny

Or will you lean, or will you look
In Jenny's pewter mirror?
Then not too long, and not so low
As make its stillness shiver
Or she will take you by the hair
To be with her forever

O never throw a wishing-pebble
Keep your wishing-penny
Her heart is empty as the sky
And angry is Fen Jenny

Or will you whistle, will you sing
To make your better cheer?
Then do not let the music sink
In Jenny's jealous ear
Or she will drag you down and down
To be her pretty dear

Beware her green and binding hair
For love she has not any
Her song is the November wind
And lonely is Fen Jenny.

The Changeling

I had three daughters, and the first two were at school,
there was only the youngest left with me at home.
Three and a half years old, she wouldn't do a thing
but what she called her 'writings', which were a lot of
zigzags, wobbly circles, little loops, shapes and dots.
Sheets and sheets of paper she filled with what she said
were 'writings', and if I'd no paper left to give her
she'd dip her finger in her drink and 'write' with that,
or breathe all over the windows and 'write' on that.

So I taught her her letters, though reception teachers
don't like them to come able to read and write,
they have to think of something for those to do
while all the others learn. Well, but I taught her
the letters, she seemed that keen, and next thing was,
she'd do, put strings of letters together any old how
and say What does it read? Mum, what does it read?
Well it doesn't read anything, it's just a jumble of letters.

And she'd sit at the table while we were having tea
and – so you've got a salad cream bottle or something –
she'd, in the air with her nose, she'd copy the letters
or the ones on the cereal box at breakfast time.
Constantly doing letters – like, obsessed. Bewitched.

White Ink

Slaap kindje slaap
Sleep baby sleep
Daar buiten loopt een schaap
Outside is a sheep
Een schaap met witte voetjes
A sheep with little white feet
drinkt zijn melk zo zoetjes
who drinks his milk so sweet

thine is the kingdom the power and the glory
mine is the crook of my mother's arm
mine the warmth and the bedtime story
under her wing and safe from harm
thine be the kingdom glory and power
so I can have this warm half hour

After they teach you how to read the words
they've still to teach you how to read the books
After you're grown, grown and flown
you build your nest wherever is best
then you must sing, sing to the young
under your wing in mother tongue
twinkle twinkle little star
whatever it is, wherever you are

Poesje mauw, kom eens gauw
ik heb lekkere melk voor jou
Puss, miaow, come here now,
I have tasty milk for you
Oh wat heerlijk smullen wij

how wonderful our feast

Helpless with Laughter

Mother would read me *The House at Pooh Corner*
When I was only so high
She in her big chair and I in my little
Straight-backed Mother and I

Once I remember us helpless with laughter
Both of us laughing so much
Neither could speak, and I fell off my chair
And all she could do was to clutch

One side of her bosom – I rolled like a barrel
A barrel of laughs on the floor
She wiped her eyes and patted her hair
And said, No more now, no more.

North Staveley Songbird

We have a big enough house that we can have a playroom
and other children who live around will come and play with us there.
Before they go home, we will have some
toast and Bovril.
Mum will be in the kitchen, and the children will say to her
       Mrs Collins, sing!
       Sing that song that makes us cry.
       Are you going to sing for us?
they say
       Please sing!
I say
       Don't pull my Mummy's skirt
and I fling out at them a bit for it.

When they are gone, my Mum says
       Etty, don't behave like that.
       These people are your guests, and you don't behave like that.

But I don't want them crowding round her pulling at her skirt, all of
them saying
       Do sing us that song, make us cry.
       Oh Danny Boy.
       Sing it, Mrs Collins, please sing it!
And, I'll take you home, Kathleen.

All wiping their eyes like this, or on their sleeves, because we don't
have tissues.

A Broken Heart or Something Like It

My first day at work, a boy a little older than me
taught me how to use the telephone
we did the stamps and letters together
and took them to the post on Surrey Street
after work we went to the library and got
books out of there, most nights. All sorts.
I just looked along the shelves.

My father died in 1944
before you were born
and mother stopped eating
she went an awful yellow colour
she couldn't eat
we didn't know
the doctor didn't know
what was wrong with her
she went into hospital
they operated
and they still couldn't find
anything wrong
so they sewed her up again
and she came back home
with pneumonia
like they often do
from hospital
so I had to look after her
she gradually got better
but she'd got down to five stone
Doctor Gunn said she'd got a broken heart.
It was something like that, anyway.

Your father used to read to us,
library books, in the evenings
when she was recovering
and I was expecting you.

He had a lovely gentle reading voice.
I remember it was *The Egg and I*
and we were busy knitting while he read;
I don't know whether men still do that.

Why Is the Skull Crying

It's funny what sticks in your mind.
In the window they had one book
on the cover there was a skull
there were pearls rolling down its face
it was called The Devil's Tears
I stood there staring at it thinking
why is the skull crying
I must have been a macabre child

I can remember being six, enunciating
A-E-I-O-U
into a little round mirror
to make sure we spoke properly
and I laughed
and got told to stand behind the blackboard

A little lost chick sang cheep in the night
Cheep in the night
And the moon stretched her arms out
Shiny and bright
To the little lost chick that sang cheep in the night.
Isn't it pathetic? So sad.

It wasn't a happy marriage. I said to her once
Mum, why did you marry him?
And she just shrugged her shoulders.
But once, she came out with 'You know,
your father never bothered me much
about That. You know.' And I sat there
40 and married with two kids,
with me mouth open. And that was that;
as though she had to wait
until I was 40 to tell me.

That's what I think the library was:
an escape. She'd not much at home.
Just used to bury her face in a book.

A Burning

I fell out with somebody once who burnt their books. It was a new
couple, getting married, and they said to me, oh, we burnt all his
books. I don't want to be friends with people who burn books.

We were a new couple just starting out,
it was none of my idea for a nice home. I saw
     Unmixt with foreign filth, and undefil'd
pale walls, made-to-measure pencil-pleat curtains
at every sparkling window; all cream carpets
     Beseeming well the bower of anie Queene.
Where could these go, so many of them
     Guilty of dust and sin
and spiders spinning behind them, I said
who's going to be pulling them forward four at a time
to do the shelves twice a week? Not me.

He wasn't best pleased. But I reasoned with him
     Till, dying, all he can resign is breath
I said well you've read them, haven't you?
Any you've read, you know what's in them.
     'Tis madness to resist or blame
Any you haven't, you obviously weren't interested,
or you would have got round to it sooner.
     Longings wild and vain
          For the rich help of books
Neither use nor ornament, and besides,
where will they go? Come on, we'll do it together.

I'm the type of person, once my mind's made up,
I want to get on with it
     And bonefiers make all day
Good thing it was a dry October
     So red, so ripe the roses burned
and he still had the allotment back then,

it took two trips in his car and all afternoon
I warm'd both hands before the fire of life
to get rid of them. It was sort of interesting
watching them catch at the edges and then go up.

Peace, good reader, do not weep

I made us a cup of tea in the shed, we shared
a packet of biscuits. I forget what kind.

Good Hunting

Certain features she could not
disguise said so, and that was that.
Plus, this town, small as it
is, boasts its own pricker. What
merry hubbub, the historic night
they tailed him hooting to her cot!

Sure enough, he found the spot,
black as a smut in the sweetest meat
of the thigh. Sure enough, he got
her with his wee pin, her and her pet
cat too. She was exposed all right.

You would have thought the ground would split
and her dirty lord come clattering bat-
winged up with a shout to get her. You'd have thought
at least she'd go off with some fizz and spit
like a firework, fountaining out
her turpitude in bursting balls of scarlet
and violet.

But no,
it was just like roasting a skinny sow.
She was an awful long while moaning, too,

before the fumes of rendered self
wreathing her like a dark scarf
choked her off.

Blood Sugar

No one gave him a scallop-shell or scrip
of anything; he worked long years for this.
He'll take his As, his hard-earned scholarship,
his knotted hankie full of prejudice,

and seek for truth among the pleasant groves
of academe (*Epistles*, Horace). Art
hangs in those trees like fruit; like geese in droves,
ideas fill those lanes. His gritstone heart

softens to each blithe spirit there chance-met,
each punting lutenist, each well-read youth,
each fortune-favoured lightfoot lad. And yet:
although all Oxford knows Beauty is Truth

and Truth is Beauty, Sheffield says 'Not quite.'
Sheffield wonders with Brecht, of what is built
the palace of culture? Such a golden white,
honey on yoghurt, syrup on cream, gilt

tears not worth spilling on milk spilt long ago.
The temple of learning glows like toffee ice.
Or sugar. Raw cane sugar. When you know
t'truth about beauty, then you question t'price.

Snatches of Old Lauds

I found my Sunday School hymn book –
the Bible in another form, we used to say;
the poetry helps you remember.
But damp in the attic had got it.
What hadn't mouldered away up there
disintegrated softly in my hands.

My memory's very bad now
but I can still remember this:
I am not skilled to understand
What God has willed and God has planned
I only know, at God's right hand
Stands one who is my Saviour.
I still find myself singing them,
words I didn't know I knew.

The Book Room, they called the headquarters
of the Wesleyan Reformed Union.
The Attercliffe chapel's still there:
it is now a mosque.
So there's probably lots of reasons
or books that might be read about that:
how it's still there, but in another form.

I looked online to see if I could buy
a copy of my old hymn book –
I should like to have it again, for the memories.
I found a thing that said
This is a digital copy of a book
that was preserved for generations on library shelves
before it was carefully scanned
and there I read (I wrote it down):

Q Hear Thmfrmn Thy dwelUng-pkice, 77.77.77.77.
even from heaven, - 2 Chronicles vl. 21.
1 rrOD of glory, God of grace,
vJ Hear from heaven, Thy dwelling-place.
While our feeble voices sing
Grateftd praises to our King.

Which isn't how I remembered it;
but I suppose it is still there
in a different form.

Heroes II

Biggles and Sapper, Bulldog Drummond – wait,
fascist alert: 'Six-six in stockinged feet,
fit as a butcher's dog, all-round good egg,
crack shot, an artist in the boxing ring,
shoulders worth two of any rowing eight...'
but ten-year-olds don't question what they read.

Best thing they ever said to me at school:
'Right, gentlemen, we've got a spare half hour.
Whoever has a book may read at will.'
Some of me mates thought I was slightly weird;
that followed me to work. About 13
I saw that I were on a different course.

Hank Janson was the books you shouldn't read
and some o't' lads would bring 'em in from home,
Whoa, look at this, she slunk in and he caught
a glimpse of silken thigh. That sort of stuff.
I don't know that I did enjoy them much,
I don't think they were written all that well.

A lot of what we read in school – I mean,
the classroom map was half pink at that time,
and books with heroes quelling natives, Hup
the values of Great Britain and all that.
Completely propagandised at 13;
we were the greatest nation on God's earth.

The Road to Wigan Pier – that was the book
opened my eyes, because he was describing
conditions we were born in, and for me
that was the dawnings of, this isn't right.
We shouldn't live like this, and let it be
dressed up as duty, or as destiny.

A Lot of Schoolboy Stories

I went to boarding school, sonny;
it never did me any harm.
More of us went on to Oxbridge
than into the 'funny farm'!

Rejected at 8 by the mater,
you jolly well learned to keep calm
when they flushed your head in the privy
and stubbed out cigars on your arm!

Elect, well-groomed, and anointed
with all your seducer's balm,
you didn't go blubbing or blabbing,
'blow whistles' or raise the alarm!

Yes, there was bullying, sonny,
and welts upon buttock and palm,
but jingo! Our grammar was solid.
It never did me any harm.

The Jig-borer

Work was getting short and people were
getting worried. He says well,
go in the army and do yer two years.
Pop in and see us when you're on leave.
Teaching drill is teaching 'em how to
polish the boots and the brasses
black all the webbing, press their battle-dresses
keep the barrack-room clean and tidy.
Training for drill-instructor is many many hours
pounding the drill square
learning to shout, learning to
shout *at* people. So that was what you did, you
got a new squad every 14 weeks
started from page 1
worked to the end of the manual. And that
was me for two years. I couldn't then go and

sit in an office, the very thought
frightened me; I wanted to
play with things,
knock lumps off pieces of metal. I was
Gauging Tool Inspector, technician-level; then I got to
operate the jig-borer. A very sophisticated piece of kit,
made in Switzerland, would have
filled this half of the room – temperature-controlled cabinet and it
worked to a ten-thousandth of an inch. They kept
feeding in these bits of metal that
wanted holes in certain places, and I
put 'em exactly where they
wanted to be. Then suddenly it had all

finished and no more overtime for the tool-room
costing too much. The job was
done.

The Tracer

I got past romances. I think you do.
Read *Lady Chatterley* when everyone
was on about it. And I thought, so what?
Perhaps for schoolgirls, wanting to find out –
but once you're married, you know what goes where,
and once you're old…consenting adults, fine,
in private, fine (her husband's private land…)

*

Looking the wrong way down a telescope
I see myself the year I'm due to take
my School Certificate. And I fall ill.
I think I might still manage, but the head
says no, you'd have to do the year again.
My mother thinks I'll be too old by then.
Marches me straight to town to get a job.

Fifteen years old, first day at Thomas Birt,
small tools department, drawing office girl.
The boss says What's your name? I say, Irene.
He says All right then, Renie. And I say
It isn't Renie, sir. My name's Irene.
He says, All right then, Renie. And that's that.

I trace the draughtsmen's drawings, then they go
to blueprints for the workshop. War breaks out.
We're told our occupation is 'reserved'.
We work long hours, now drawing blades that cut
the cords of sea-mines, aircraft engine parts.
I wed the nicest youngest draughtsman there.

*

I got past romance novels pretty young.
The same with Catherine Cookson, I got bored;
someone is (whisper) *illegitimate*.
Again: so what? They're also fictional.
Hard to see how it matters either way.

Blue Rain

In 1940-whatever-it-is
                    we get bombed out, so we move.
By the time I'm nine, my mother has died
                    and the three of us are split up:
I go to Ripon, the children's home
                    the twins are sent to Diss
that's the last we see of each other
                    for three and a half more years.
Dad, in the army in Africa,
                    is not allowed to come back
not even for Mother's funeral.
                    But when he gets out, he comes
almost just as I've always dreamed
                    turns up at the children's home
to take me away, to fetch the twins
                    all safe together again.

Only, before the end of the war,
                    he'd married this lady in Belgium.
She was to come and live with us too.
                    She didn't like me to read.
As soon as she saw me pick up a book
                    she'd find me a job to do.
I used to stand by my window to read
                    as long as there was light.
Some of it helped me to understand –
                    people, and how they are.
Some, if I read for evermore,
                    I'd still not understand.

War Quartet

I

He'd no need to go up in the war, but he did,
for some reason, he volunteered.

Of course, he was wounded in 1917.
Three of them, captain, sergeant, and him
they used to put the wires,
used to go out at night and put the wires

They both got killed, and he was left
in a shell-hole all night long
until they came and got him out
but he got gangrene,
had to have the leg off to there

He never talked about it.
Only when we had the blitz here
and we had to go down to the cellar at night
you could see it in his face.

II

When they got married, she lived at Highfields
she'd just got my brother then, a baby,
and she wouldn't stop on her own
when he went up
she was one of those people,
she would not stop
in the house on her own

She went back to her mother's
gave her house up
and went home
so they never went back
to that side of town
when he came back from war.

III

My husband volunteered in 1939
fancied himself as a naval engineer

but he had a good war
not like some of those other poor people
he had a lovely time

four years cruising on a battleship
Australia and Japan
so he wasn't interested in travelling
when he got back
he'd done all that.

IV

When they came with the incendiary bombs
they were coming for the steelworks
but they missed
dropped them on the canal side

I should have stayed on at school to 15
but everything stopped, so I left
they didn't bother with girls then
boys could have anything, but you get married

that was the attitude
and it was true
so we didn't get anywhere.

Bledewort

We are field poppy, thunder flower, corn rose
common and widespread
corn poppy, Klatschmohn, coquelicot
not of conservation concern
common poppy, red weed, headwark

our habitat is anywhere disturbed
papaver rhoeas, paper rose
in barleyfields, battlefields, roadsides
bledewort, blood-root, bleed word
on any waste land

red poppy, Flanders poppy, headache,
we are a weed, we are a proud
bright red abundant annual weed
so many among the wheat
we might be mistaken for a crop

but in cornfields, battlefields, roadsides,
waste land and other disturbed places
we are red weed, bleed word, common
poppy.

*

Being, we sing.
Nothing being lacks its song

*

Song of the wind in the poppies
petals creased in the bud
like the letter she made a fist round
when it came back unread

song of the wind in the petals
crumpled flags in the field
song of the seventh magpie
a secret not to be told

song of the wind on the seed pods
a dry whisper within
of songs that are too soon ended
or never begin

*

We are the never-were, we are
children who only might have been
dream children of the spinster aunts
and lost or killed or broken men

leaves once or twice pinnately lobed
the petals crumpled in the bud
an inkling on the edge of sleep
four rounded petals bright as blood

the showy scarlet flowers nod
on slender greyish hirsute stalks
abundant on the roadsides where
they took their evening courtship walks

papery petals overlap
a dark blotch often at the base
his head-wound stained the bandages
her loss forever bruised her face

the male parts numerous, black anthers
borne on thin black filaments
the stigma, darkly open mouth
of disappointed innocence

flowers appear in June, July
so red the fields it seems a rush
of blood, and after harvest time
between sheared stalks, a second flush

anthers dehisce while still in bud;
self-pollination can occur,
one plant produce four hundred blooms.
She dreamed of five who never were.
He closed his eyes and dreamed of her.

In bloom, the two free sepals fall,
The crumpled scarlet petals spread.
The fruit, a smooth and hairless globe
the black seeds ripen and are shed

to sleep a painless poppy sleep
but dream a vivid poppy dream
of fallen men and maiden aunts
and all their children
and all their children might have been.

Chess Queen's Letters Home

I didn't want to wake you when I left.
You looked so noble sleeping, maybe dreaming
of ceasefire, treaty, truce and peace at last,
a statesman's compromise, a here and now
of happy children singing. I was deft
in dressing, seeing ceaseless whitefire gleaming
on polished steel, and paused before I passed
to kiss the air an inch above your brow.

Don't be too angry. All I took's
a knife to slip inside my boot,
last birthday's triple row of pearls
and one fond backward look at you.
The blade because there's work to do;
the necklace – well, girls will be girls;
the glance, the only thing I shoot.
I left the crown, and all your books.

It didn't take me long
around a mile-high noon
I heard the soldier's song
We go to battle soon
They do look splendid, dear
firm jaws and ramrod spines
the most tremendous cheer
as I rode down the lines

the mud, the gear,
the din, the smell,
the blood, the fear,
the sin – the hell,

One of us has to do it, and it's me.
You'll miss me as the pensive ocean misses
one silver thought a diving bird has speared,
I'll miss you as the raincloud does the sea
that sighs it out. I send my warmest kisses
to nestle in your grave patrician beard.

     *

War is an Education
isn't it Sire
yesterday for instance
I met some young
ladies travelling towards
camp. I asked them
why. They said they
were going to Entertain
the Troops. Are you,
I said, What sort of
Entertainment
would that be?
Contemporary Dance
said one, and they all
laughed a good deal;
they seemed a super
cheerful bunch.
However, morale among
our men happens
to be quite high
owing to the success
of an idea I had to
sabotage the other
side's siege engines.
So, one working girl
to another, I told them
they should go and
Entertain
the other troops

instead, and gave them
a string of pearls
between them
for their trouble.
It was lucky I did this,
as it turns out the
fungal and bacterial
consequences of
watching too much
Contemporary Dance
can be surprisingly
debilitating: our boys
have all been
Warned Off it.
Sorry about writing
on bandage, no paper.
Kisses, Wife.

*

Darling, you know the Bishops you sent? Have you got another two?
Because ours and theirs decided to have this Ecumenical Do
In No Man's Land, where they'd pray for peace and concelebrate a Mass
(they groan in foreign for hours and hours, with clouds of sweet-smelling gas,
but the choir is good, and I dress in black with your Mother's Valenciennes
        lace)
and there comes this bit where they do a thing with some bells, and say a
        grace,
or it might be a toast, and they take a break for a little drink of wine
and a cracker they snap in bits to share. Well, normally this goes fine,
but Sunday, nobody knows for sure was it something wrong with the bread
or something wrong with the wine, but well! they all just fell down dead.
I thought we might manage without for a while, but it seems that men at
        war
prefer to have some religion around, so do please send some more.

*

Darling, in haste:
this Grandmama's fail-safe recipe.
in biggest cauldrons, all cooking and other household fats –
olive oil, sunflower, Marseilles soap from laundry,
beef dripping (Cook will help) etc.
Bring to a rolling boil.
Add sack of sugar – do not omit,
v important ingredient,
mixture will not adhere properly without.
When enemy arrives at gate, send down
expendable eg convicted criminal
to say 'Come on in, we surrender.'
Ensure all enemy cavalry safely inside
milling around shouting.
Drop gate.
In a steady stream, pour fat/sugar mix;
flambé at once (flaming arrows good for this).
If done right, should have
appalling scene unnecessary suffering plus
ineradicable stench fried caramel horse.

      *

On my way home.
Nice hot bath, large glass of wine
ready please. Thanks,
Love,
Wife.

Poem on the Underground

The tube-mice sway and shimmy like a stream of charcoal
wine up the dirty escalator where the sun's too shy to shine
the commuters dance a samba sinuous and serpentine when
they drink a little quatrain and remember life is fine all the
skinny weeny tube-mice boogie up into the street and the muted
charcoal-suited with intoxicated feet dance a tantalising tango
with a supple sultry beat when they drink a little quatrain and
remember life is sweet well perhaps it doesn't happen but I'd
like it understood that some charcoal shoes are shuffled while
they wonder if they should and they smile to think about it
and that's nearly just as good.

ACKNOWLEDGEMENTS

Acknowledgements for sponsorship funding are due to the following: Sylvia Dunkley, Mary and Derek Grover, Loveday Herridge, Judith and Steve Loveman, Kate McCullough, Frances Soar, Eleanor Watts and Sheffield Hallam University.